AF278474

MASTERING

STUDY GUIDE

JOSHUA D. ROWE

CONTENTS

INTRODUCTION:

If you've already picked up a copy of "Mastering Life before It's Too Late", this workbook is for you. This workbook is meant to be a supplementary resource, so if you don't yet have a book, check out robertjmorgan.com where you can purchase a copy of this and other titles by Robert J. Morgan.

If you're interested in group study, check out the Mastering Life video training series, taught by Robert J. Morgan at robertjmorgan.com/masteringlifetraining. This resource is perfect for church small groups, employee training, church staff training, college groups, and individuals.

My name is Joshua Rowe, and Robert Morgan has been my mentor for years. Having seen Robert masterfully apply these patterns, and having been his student for over a decade, Rob asked me to put together this workbook to assist you on your journey of *Mastering Life Before It's Too Late*.

Because of my close relationship with the author (and by extension, yours as you walk through his material), please note that throughout this workbook we'll refer to him as 'Pastor Morgan', 'Robert', or just 'Rob', so don't let it throw you off!

If you've read any of Pastor Morgan's books, you already know his writing is distinctive in that he's a Bible teacher. Scripture has so permeated every aspect of his life, it oozes out onto every page. That's why the book you're about to study is so powerful. When it comes to managing your life, there's no lack of self-help books to get you organized and productive. But Rob's perspective is uniquely derived from Scripture, which offers an unmatched approach to understanding your life, your purpose, and how to live effectively. In the introduction, Robert writes:

> *We believe we're on this planet for a reason, but most people can't figure out what that is…We search everywhere for ways to improve, yet the only truly effective life is one unapologetically woven from the strands of Scripture. That's what this book is about.*

In the book, Pastor Morgan will guide you through ten Scriptural patterns, building a foundation to help you live more effectively in the time you've been given. To enhance the impact of his teaching, this workbook is primarily aimed at three things:

1. To help emphasize and further explore key ideas

2. To prompt self-analysis to help identify areas for improvement

3. To challenge you towards practical application of patterns

To accomplish these objectives, the workbook is divided into ten sections—one for each pattern you'll discover in Robert's book. Each pattern will give us a chance to interact in three key ways, with space allotted in this workbook to write responses and notes:

- **EXPLORE**: True to form, Pastor Morgan bases his principles on Scripture. We'll look at key ideas and explore passages to get a fuller sense of each pattern.

- **REFLECT**: In the Bible, James tells us that Scripture is much like a mirror, meant to show us what's true about ourselves. As we look at biblical principles, we should always reflect on our own lives: habits, attitudes, patterns, etc. Blanks will be provided for self-analysis to help you identify areas for improvement.

- **APPLY**: Reading *Mastering Life before It's Too Late* is worthless without putting the patterns into practice. You'll be challenged to apply what you read throughout this workbook, and to interact and respond to these challenges.

- **APPLYING BALANCE**: This will not appear in every section. However, there are some dangers in diving into this type of material. If we're overzealous or wrongly apply the patterns, we can become robotic, workaholics, or overwhelmed with too many principles. These "applying balance" statements will help maintain a balanced approach.

Since Robert typically breaks each of the ten biblical patterns down into sections, we'll usually break our study up likewise to cover the same ground in the same order.

This workbook includes quite a variety of material. Some sections are heavily weighted towards bible study while others are almost completely application. Some include links to downloadable files to help you get started on practical portions of this material. Some will ask you to have a calendar out and ready. Others require a Bible and end with prayer. That's what makes this book, and workbook, unique: we want to allow Scripture to guide us into practice; so that's our aim in this journey.

> ****IMPORTANT NOTE:** *These three features (Explore, Reflect, Apply) will not be divided into three distinct parts per section. Instead we'll weave in and out of these items throughout. For example, we might explore a passage, reflect on it, and suggest application—then do it all again for the next passage or key principle. On the other hand, we may spend an entire section on exploring and reflecting, only to move to the next section that contains 100% application.*

All Scripture quoted is NIV, unless otherwise noted.

> *"Success is doing the will of God and doing it with the right attitudes and one-day increments as He assigns the work—being synchronized with the sacred."*
> *–Robert J. Morgan*

The First Pattern:

LISTEN TO A TWELVE-YEAR-OLD

"Why did you seek me? Did you not know that I must be about My Father's business?"
–Luke 2:49; NKJV

Before moving on, read the first pattern (all three sections) from Mastering Life Before It's Too Late.

Pastor Morgan breaks pattern one down into three main sections. In a sentence or two below each, write in your own words what each means:

1. First Words, Last Words

_____

_____

2. Just for Today

_____

_____

3. The Most Pleasant Life Anyone Can Live

_____

_____

Let's look at each section:

1. First Words, Last Words

EXPLORE: Read **Luke 2:41–52**. From the time Jesus was a child, He had a sense of God's divine purpose on His life. He couldn't conceive of being anywhere else than the Father's house, doing anything else but the Father's work. How do you think that perspective affected His ministry?

_____

_____

_____

REFLECT: Do you wake up each day with a sense of divine purpose so strong that you can't conceive of doing anything else? Why do you or why don't you believe this to be true in your life?

_____

_____

_____

EXPLORE: Read John 19:30 and John 17:4. At the end of Jesus' life, He had a sense of accomplishment, that He had successfully finished the work His Father had given Him to do. Why do you think he was so confident?

_____

_____

_____

REFLECT: If you knew that today would be your last, could you confidently say you've accomplished the work God has allotted for you? Why do you or don't you believe this to be true of you?

_____

_____

_____

_____

APPLYING BALANCE: As we approach this concept of divine purpose, it's important not to load ourselves down with unnecessary guilt, assuming the only true ministry is vocational, or what's traditionally considered "ministry". Robert tells a story about a young man who was discouraged, feeling useless working a job that wasn't in ministry. If you tend to feel discouraged about your current vocation, be encouraged by Rob's advice to this young man:

> _...don't worry about it. Right now the phone company has hired you to be a minister on their staff, and they're paying your ministerial salary...You are surrounded all day by customers and employees who need a smile, a bit of hope, an encouraging word, wise counsel, and the witness of a godly life. As time goes by, you'll find ways of sharing your faith..._

APPLY: Rob writes that the difference between someone who can say these things with Christ, and someone who can't, is often a decision: "The decision to adopt God's will for yourself is a lifetime, life-long choice, and it's the only true starting place for mastering life." He continues by offering this challenge:

> On the basis of God's mercy and Christ's cross, you can determine now, at this moment, to offer yourself as a living sacrifice, transformed, living out God's will and determined to be pleasantly productive for Him during your remaining minutes, days, and years on earth. It's as simple as saying, "Yes, Lord!"

Here's a prayer from the book you can offer right now:

> There are many things I can do in life, I have many possible venues and avenues, many options and opportunities, many decisions and distractions. But Christ gave me a pattern to follow, and He died to provide eternal life. Under His lordship, I pledge to live for Him, to devote myself to the Father's business from this moment and forever. I want to find and fulfill God's unique docket and destiny for my life, whatever it means—just like Jesus.

2. Just for Today

EXPLORE: For our purposes, we might re-state the pattern "Listen to a Twelve-Year Old" to mean: "Understand, like Jesus, that your life has a divine purpose." However, this pattern would be incomplete without the next facet Robert discusses:

> Our Father's business may consume our lifetimes, but we can't just think of it in lifelong terms. Having made an abiding decision to commit ourselves to the lordship of Christ and the will of God, we must then reduce it to bite-size realities, which we call "days." With the trajectory of our lives aligned Godward, we can faithfully implement this attitude on a daily basis.

REFLECT: Throughout the chapter, Pastor Morgan gives many examples of well-known, faithful Christians who lived according to the idea of taking life one day at a time, waking to engage God's work for the day and going to bed reflecting on what was done for the Lord. Are you approaching today in this way? Explain your perspective and how, if applicable, it needs adjusting:

APPLY: Read Colossians 3:23. Based on your agenda for today, write this verse as it applies. Below you'll re-write "Whatever you do, work at it with all your heart, as working for the Lord, not human masters", filling in the blanks with tasks you have today. For example: "Today, when you [replace shingles, do dishes, file paperwork, give a presentation, etc.] work at it with all your heart..."

Today, when you

_____   _____

_____   _____

_____   _____

work at it with all your heart, as working for the Lord, not for human masters.

EXPLORE: Rob points out several occurrences of the phrase "One thing" in Scripture. Why do you think these passages are significant?

_____

_____

_____

_____

REFLECT: Robert asserts that planning is indeed a good thing. However, he notes that we can plan our lives days, weeks, or months ahead, but we really don't know much about what will happen very far into the future. Do you struggle with being haphazard about your time, or are you an over-planner? How should you adjust your perspective based on what you've read in this section?

_____

_____

_____

_____

APPLY: At the end of this section, Robert notes that: "The secret to being effective, efficient, and effervescent is this biblical truth: God has a specific purpose for our lives, and when we turn aside from all else to follow God's plan, we synchronize with the sacred." He also notes:

> *We may not be able to contend with a decade all at once, or joust with a year, or even manage a month. But we can tackle today. Just for today we can be pleasantly productive. Just for today we can be faithful. Just for today we can resist temptation. Just for today we can choose to be joyful and to live for Jesus. Just for today we can be about the Father's business.*

Write a list of your own "Just for today:" statements below.

Just for today, I can:

_____

_____

_____

_____

3. The Most Pleasant Life Anyone Can Live

REFLECT: Pastor Morgan argues that: "You may be the hardest-working, most productive person in the world, but if you're not living on purpose, you're caught in a relentless drift. If you're doing the wrong things, it's a life poorly spent." Would you describe your life as one of purpose, doing the *right* kinds of things? Explain your answer:

_____

_____

_____

_____

EXPLORE: Read Titus 3:14. How does this Scripture emphasize Rob's statement above?

_____

_____

_____

_____

REFLECT: Robert warns that: "Many people waste mindless hours surfing the internet, playing computer and video games, watching TV, going to movies, engaging in idle chitchat, and frittering away their lives on nothing more than diversions." Write a list below of the top five time wasters in your life:

1. _____

2. _____

3. _____

4. _____

5. _____

APPLY: Below, write out a "just for today" plan to avoid or scale back on these activities:

_____

_____

_____

_____

APPLYING BALANCE: It's important to note that later in the book, Pastor Morgan gives full weight to the importance and necessity of leisurely, personal, and restful activities. So don't be discouraged at your list of "distractions"—and only list these things that aren't part of your purposeful routine of rest, relaxation, and physical health.

My Summary of Pattern One:

In this workbook, at the beginning of this pattern, I asked you to explain the meaning behind each section's title. Here's how I would re-word them: "Understand, like Jesus, that your life has a divine purpose and you will live a life that is successful in God's eyes." Second: "Living this way means not over-emphasizing the past or the future, even though it's helpful to both reflect and plan. Instead, live each day with the attitude that God has planned and equipped you for this 24-hour period, and you can accomplish the work He has for you." And finally, this section teaches us, "Living your life with a divine sense of purpose in daily units is only achievable through a life redeemed by Christ, which means a life of God's work instead of time-wasting diversions, and it's the most pleasant life possible."

Now that you've completed this section, would you agree with my summary? How would you re-word what you've learned differently? Use the space below to explain:

_____

_____

_____

_____

_____

_____

_____

_____

_____

_____

_____

_____

The Second Pattern:

REDEEM THE TIME

"Teach us to number our days, that we may gain a heart of wisdom"
–Psalm 90:12; NKJV

"Look carefully then how you walk, not as unwise but as wise, making the best use of the time, because the days are evil."
–Ephesians 5:15–16; ESV

Before moving on, read the second pattern (all four sections) from Mastering Life Before It's Too Late.

Robert breaks pattern two down into four main sections.

Let's look at each section:

1. Life is Just a Minute

In this section, Rob says "Until we appreciate the value of time and learn to manage it with skill, we can never manage ourselves." This statement sets up the second pattern. In other words, in this section your goal is to align your perspective on time with Scripture, and to implement practices to manage time better.

EXPLORE: Read John 9:1–6, paying close attention to every word of verse 4. What do you notice about Jesus' perspective on time, and how it should be used?

_____

_____

_____

REFLECT: Pastor Morgan offers a unique perspective on time, saying: "Management of time is our greatest stewardship, even greater than the stewardship of our money." Is this explanation encouraging or discouraging, based on how you've treated your time up to this point? How can you improve? Explain below:

_____

_____

_____

EXPLORE: As in the previous pattern, Robert warns against time wasters. This time, though, he divides this into three main categories: misdirection (doing the wrong things), laziness (being overcome by lethargy), and entertainment (being addicted to diversions). Which of these categories does Morgan argue to be the most pervasive in our culture? Which of these does he argue is the most satanic?

_____

_____

_____

_____

REFLECT: Which of these categories do you struggle with the most?

_____

_____

_____

_____

APPLY: Write out a prayer below, committing every moment God has given you to His service, even in the mundane things of life. Confess areas that have distracted you and ask for His strength to re-focus:

_____

_____

_____

_____

2. The Bible's Twin Texts on Time

As we identified before, our purpose in this pattern is to shift our perspective and to build strategies and skills to better manage our time.

Rob highlights what he calls the "Bible's Twin Text on Time". This section, then, will help us further gain a biblical perspective on managing our time in order to be properly grounded and motivated for putting strategies and techniques into practice.

EXPLORE: Read all of Psalm 90. Answer the following:

- What's the significance of Moses as the author? How does that affect your reading of this text?

  _____

  _____

- Does this text encourage or discourage you? Why?

  _____

  _____

- Did you notice, as Robert points out, the juxtaposition of God as eternal (unlimited by time) next to the finite earthly lives of humans? How does this affect your approach to managing your time?

  _____

  _____

REFLECT: Verse 10 tells us "Our days may come to seventy years, or eighty, if our strength endures; yet the best of them are but trouble and sorrow, for they quickly pass, and we fly away." Does this make you look forward to eternity? Worried about how effective your life is now? Sad at how quickly time passes? Explain below:

_____

_____

_____

_____

APPLICATION: The book mentions that this verse led Moses, and should lead us, to an important prayer. Take a moment to recite this verse, and Robert's rephrasing of it, as a prayer:

"Teach us to number our days, that we may gain a heart of wisdom."
—Psalm 90:12.

As Rob rephrases:

"Lord, keep me from wasting time. Since You are infinite and my life on earth is brief, teach me to count each day and to make each day count. May I be a good steward of every moment. May I number my days like a miser counting his coins. When You look at my usage of time, may You see a heart of wisdom."

EXPLORE: Read Ephesians 5:15–17 and answer the following:

■ In Paul's time, he described the days as "evil". Do you think that's still true today? If so, what makes you think so?

_____

_____

■ How does "redeeming the time" make a difference in the context of evil days?

_____

_____

■ The book points out that, while Psalm 90 is a prayer, this verse is a command. Why is that significant?

_____

_____

REFLECT: If you were to compare your schedule as a Christian, to that of someone who lives according to the wisdom of this world, how would yours be different? In what ways should it be distinctive?

_____

_____

_____

APPLY: Pastor Morgan summarizes:

When we're about our Father's business, we're to number our days, for life is swift; we're to redeem the time for the days are evil. But in God's perfectly designed plan, there is always enough work for the days He has given us, and exactly enough days for the work He has assigned.

How do you plan to apply what you've learned from this mini Bible study on the Bible's "twin texts on time"?

_____

_____

_____

APPLYING BALANCE: As you apply these principles, be careful not to become obsessive. Heed Pastor Morgan's warning as he writes:

> *It's possible to be overly obsessive about anything, and sometimes in our split-second world, we take time-consciousness to extremes. I once saw these words posted on a bulletin board: "Blessed are the flexible, for they shall not get bent out of shape."*

3. Living Clockwise

The previous two sections of this pattern are heavy in terms of Bible study and reflection. These latter two sections weigh more heavily towards practical application of these principles. So have your calendar out and use this section for notes as we attempt to build strategies and skills to better manage our time.

The Focus Block Method

APPLICATION: At the beginning of this section, Robert explains his process of charting out the hours he has in a typical week (often referred to as the focus-block method". If you've not done this before, do so now. A sample image of what this may look like is below.

	Monday	Tuesday	Wednesday	Thursday	Friday	Saturday	Sunday
5:00 AM	SLEEP	SLEEP	SLEEP	SLEEP	SLEEP	SLEEP	SLEEP
6:00 AM	Quiet Time	Quiet Time	Quiet Time	Quiet Time	Quiet Time	SLEEP	SLEEP
7:00 AM	Exercise / Shower	Exercise / Shower	Exercise / Shower	Exercise / Shower	Exercise / Shower	Quiet Time	Quiet Time
8:00 AM	Drive / Book on Tape	Drive / Book on Tape	Drive / Book on Tape	Drive / Book on Tape	Drive / Book on Tape	Exercise / Shower	Shower
9:00 AM	WORK	WORK	WORK	WORK	WORK	Yardwork	CHURCH
10:00 AM	WORK	WORK	WORK	WORK	WORK	Yardwork	CHURCH
11:00 AM	WORK	WORK	WORK	WORK	WORK	Yardwork	CHURCH
12:00 PM	WORK	WORK	WORK	WORK	WORK	Friends/Family Time	Friends/Family Time
1:00 PM	WORK	WORK	WORK	WORK	WORK	Friends/Family Time	Friends/Family Time
2:00 PM	WORK	WORK	WORK	WORK	WORK	Study Time	Friends/Family Time
3:00 PM	WORK	WORK	WORK	WORK	WORK	Friends/Family Time	Friends/Family Time
4:00 PM	WORK	WORK	WORK	WORK	WORK	Friends/Family Time	Friends/Family Time
5:00 PM	WORK	WORK	WORK	WORK	WORK	Friends/Family Time	Friends/Family Time
6:00 PM	Drive / Book on Tape	Drive / Book on Tape	Drive / Book on Tape	Drive / Book on Tape	Drive / Book on Tape	Friends/Family Time	CHURCH
7:00 PM	Friends/Family Time	Friends/Family Time	Friends/Family Time	CHURCH	Date Night	Friends/Family Time	CHURCH
8:00 PM	Friends/Family Time	Friends/Family Time	Friends/Family Time	CHURCH	Date Night	Friends/Family Time	Friends/Family Time
9:00 PM	Friends/Family Time	Friends/Family Time	Friends/Family Time	Friends/Family Time	Date Night	Friends/Family Time	Friends/Family Time
10:00 PM	SLEEP	SLEEP	SLEEP	SLEEP	SLEEP	SLEEP	SLEEP
11p–4a	SLEEP	SLEEP	SLEEP	SLEEP	SLEEP	SLEEP	SLEEP

You can also download a free spreadsheet here to get started: *robertjmorgan.com/downloads/focusblock.xls* – or download the google doc here: *http://goo.gl/A8f5HP* – This document is a very simple starter file you should heavily modify to fit your own plan.

You can also simply use graph paper or create your own grid on a simple 8.5 x 11 sheet.

Once you have this or a similar document, be sure to do the following:

- Block out non-negotiables (these may be work hours, class periods, meetings, etc.).

- While working on this schedule, keep in mind the book's important comment:

  - What is important in life? Time for prayer, Bible study, reading, thinking, and soul refreshment; time with our spouse; time with our children or grandchildren; time to rest; time for working on those major projects that will establish our legacy.

  - The book also mentions the 30/30 plan—spending thirty minutes a day for thirty days on something important that needs work. You may want to apply this to your marriage, to important family members, to exercise, or to another important activity you've neglected. Plug 30 minutes into your weekly schedule for this plan if you so desire.

Once you've developed this skeleton, you should use it on a weekly basis. Each week comes with its own set of challenges that may require tweaking of what's typical—but it helps to have this starting point.

On a personal note, my wife and I both use Google Calendars. We've shared our calendars with each other. This way, when I'm scheduling a work-related trip, a meeting, planning to work overtime, etc. I can consult her schedule to be sure nothing conflicts with our home life. In the same way, she checks mine before making any major commitments. Pastor Morgan and his wife, in earlier days before her Multiple Schlerosis advanced, used to have coffee every Saturday and do what they called "merging calendars". For families, this can be an essential habit.

Backwards Goal Setting

APPLICATION: Now that we've looked at a typical weekly schedule, this forms the template we can use each week. But we don't want to neglect major projects. With your calendar at hand, let's apply the "backwards goal setting" strategy. Robert explains it this way:

> *If I have a project due on, say, December 15, I look at my yearly calendar and, breaking down the project into its logical components, insert the deadlines into my schedule in advance.*

With this in mind, work on the following:

- Be sure to block off major events like family vacations, surgeries, days of rest / meditation, church retreats, or anything else that needs to be in mind as you plan out projects.

- Take a few moments to put major projects on your calendar, starting with their deadline and working backwards to insert any intermediate components or milestones.

4. Gather the Fragments that Remain

Now that we've built a biblical basis for appreciating time, we've taken practical steps to better manage our calendar with appropriate priorities in place. This principle, however, helps us to maximize our effectiveness by ensuring no moment spare goes to waste.

EXPLORE: Read John 6:1–14 taking special note of verses 12 and 13. If Jesus was careful not to waste any food, and to teach His disciples that God abundantly provides, how should we apply this principle to our approach to time management?

_____

_____

_____

_____

REFLECT: How are you currently using your "spare moments"?

_____

_____

_____

APPLYING BALANCE: The book makes an important statement to help us balance our approach:

> *I might struggle some with workaholism, but I'm not advocating constant busyness. Sometimes we need to stay in the recliner, mute the commercials, and rest our nerves. I simply want us to think of the value of each passing moment.*

APPLICATION: The book also points out some of the tremendous impact that can occur when we gather up these spare moments:

> *It only takes a moment to hug a loved one, to write a thank-you note, to scan an article, to read a paragraph, to whisper a prayer, to wash a dish, to file a paper, to smile at a stranger, to cuddle a baby, to rest your eyes, to conceive an idea, to learn the next word of a verse, to straighten a pillow, to text a message of encouragement.*

Make a list of things that would only take a moment, but would have an impact on you or someone else this week. You can use the space below, or write these items in the margins on your calendar.

This week, it would only take a moment to:

- _____

- _____

- _____

- _____

- _____

- _____

- _____

The Third Pattern:

CLEAR THE DECKS

"God is not a God of confusion...[Therefore] all things must be done properly and in an orderly manner."
–1 Corinthians 14:33, 40: NASV.

Before moving on, read the third pattern (all three sections) from Mastering Life Before It's Too Late.

Pastor Morgan breaks pattern three down into three main sections. The first helps us understand from Scripture that God is orderly, which sets the precedent that we should be too. The second section teaches us to de-clutter and have everything in its place. The final section encourages us to use lists and systems by which we can organize our tasks.

Let's look at each section:

1. God Is Not Disorganized—Why Are You?

"A cluttered workspace creates a confused mind". That's the essence of this principle. But before we get to methodologies on de-cluttering and getting organized, we need to build from a biblical framework.

EXPLORE: In this section, Robert uses extensive biblical references to illuminate one central idea: that God is orderly. Let's interact with some of these passages and concepts:

- Read 1 Corinthians 14:33–40, focusing on verses 33 and 40. In the context of church life, why does it matter that God isn't a God of confusion?

_____

_____

- Pastor Morgan cites Jesus' methodical organization of the five thousand into organized groups of fifties and hundreds. How does this help us build a biblical precedent for being organized in our own lives?

_____

_____

- Read John 20:1–7. Do you think it's overreaching to interpret verse 7 as an act of Jesus putting things in order, almost like one makes a bed? How does this passage impact your understanding of Christ's orderliness?

_____

_____

- The book goes into a lot of detail about how much attention and time is given to organizing the people of Israel in order to prepare them to become a working nation before they even took hold of the land. Rob explains that God organizes churches, angels, and the Bible—that these things emanate from His very being, which is organized in the trinity. What else can you think of, from Scripture, that shows God's organizing work?

_____

_____

Here's an excellent summary from Pastor Morgan:

> *My primary point isn't to tell you to be organized or how to achieve it. Lots of books and articles do that…The contribution I'd like to make to the discussion is to emphasize* **why** *we crave an organized life. It's because our Creator is organized in His very nature, and He has built efficient organizational structures and systems into all He has done.*

APPLY: Pastor Morgan encourages us to think of all areas of our lives—"your finances, bank statements, work areas, closet, kitchen, car, desk—and say these words: 'God is not a God of confusion, therefore all things must be done properly and in an orderly manner.'" Write a list of such areas that need this kind of attention in your life, and ways you plan to address them:

- _____

- _____

- _____

- _____

- _____

- _____

APPLY: The book challenges us with application at the very end of this section. I'll re-state it here and give you space below to write in your response: "What little area of life can you tackle today? Where is the first obvious place for you to start in bringing order and function to your day?"

_____

_____

2. Put Your Tray Tables in Their Upright Positions

If the point of the first section is to build a theology of God's organization, then I would categorize the next two sections like this: "De-clutter and organize your stuff" and "Organize your tasks". This section, then, primarily focuses on physical organization, which has a surprising impact on our efficiency and psychology.

APPLICATION: The book makes several very practical points. To consolidate these, I'll list them below. Underline or highlight items you need to work on, and use the empty bullet points to add other similar items:

- Make your bed each morning (from previous chapter, but applies here).
- Clear your desk after every task.
- Empty your dishwasher.
- Sort your mail.
- File your receipts.
- Return your books to their place.
- Empty your in-box.
- Hang your keys on the hook.
- Put the bathroom towel back on the rack.
- Put the dishes back on their shelves.
- Put the tools back in the box.
- Keep the flashlight in the bed-side drawer.
- _____
- _____
- _____
- _____
- _____

"A place for everything, and everything in its place."

APPLICATION: If you're clearing out the clutter after each task, singularly focusing on the task at hand—what should you do with things that are "out of place"? Rob says: "The 'clean space' philosophy includes throwing things away and reducing clutter." Use the space below to identify areas you need to de-clutter. Then grab your calendar and schedule a time when you'll tackle these items.

_____

_____

_____

_____

Be sure to keep in mind Pastor Morgan's comments: "During this process, it's important to set up receptacles so everything has its logical place. We need to design places for everything so we'll know where it is."

APPLYING BALANCE: Keep in mind Rob's words: "Too much organization becomes counterproductive because we can't keep it up. Everything should be done with minimal complexity and maximum simplicity"

3. Don't Be Listless

Now that we've established that God is orderly, we've made plans and taken steps towards organizing our things. Now we need to be sure this process is followed through in terms of tasks. Here's the essence of this section as stated in the book:

> *We can't remember all the things we need to do. We can't intuitively do them in the proper sequence or priority. We need checklists— some way of recording our obligations, thoughts, ideas, tasks, and everything else that weighs on our minds.*

EXPLORE: Pastor Morgan says that the Lord seems to love checklists. He mentions:

- The Ten Commandments (Exodus 20:1–17)

- The nine attitudes that characterize the citizens of His kingdom (Matthew 5:2–12)

- The nine fold list of the fruits of the Spirit (Galatians 5:22–23)

Can you think of other "lists" in the Bible? Explain below:

_____

_____

_____

_____

REFLECT: Carefully read Proverbs 14:8, 15 and 21:29. Use the space below to re-word these verses into a sentence or two, using personal language. For example, you might re-write "The wisdom of the prudent is to give thought to their ways" to say something like "I should be wise by thinking more thoroughly through what I'm doing."

_____

_____

_____

REFLECT: The book tells the story of a farmer who gets distracted in each task he attempts by another that needs to be done. Does this apply to you? Keep Rob's words in mind: "Before dismissing the farmer as mindless, ask yourself, *How much of my day was spent reacting to random events as they occurred rather than pressing ahead with a definite agenda...*". How could lists help you improve?

_____

_____

_____

_____

APPLYING BALANCE: Rob notes that not everything belongs on a list. He also adds this important statement: "…the essence of what I'm saying is simple. Lists are biblical. Lists are basic. We have to keep them simple, but with a bit of thought we can use them more effectively than we think."

The Fourth Pattern:
MAXIMIZE THE MORNING

Let the morning bring me word of your unfailing love, for I have put my trust I you. Show me the way I should go.
Psalm 143:8

Before moving on, read the fourth pattern (all four sections) from Mastering Life Before It's Too Late.

Robert breaks pattern four down into four main sections, all centered around the importance of scheduled time with the Lord each day.

Let's look at each section:

1. Awake My Soul, and with the Sun

Pastor Morgan teaches "The most important thing about our day is beginning it with a spirit of doxology. If we get started on the right foot, we'll be ahead of the game all day long."

EXPLORE: The heroes of Scripture understood the importance of this. Robert spends several pages giving examples of this. Which ones resonated with you the most and why?

_____

_____

_____

_____

REFLECT: What steps should you take to be sure you begin each day with attitudes and actions of praise and thanksgiving?

_____

_____

_____

_____

APPLY: Pastor Morgan quotes the Doxology, one of our oldest English hymns. Take a moment right now, or at the beginning of your next day, to sing this hymn. If you don't know the tune, you can find it here: http://www.cyberhymnal.org/htm/p/r/praisegf.htm

Here's the entire text:

Awake my soul, and with the sun
Thy daily stage of duty run;
Shake off dull sloth, and joyful rise,
To pay thy morning sacrifice.

Direct, control, suggest this day,
All I design, or do, or say,
That all my powers, with all their might,
In Thy sole glory may unite.

Praise God, from whom all blessings flow;
Praise Him, all creatures here below;
Praise Him above, ye heavenly host;
Praise Father, Son, and Holy Ghost.

2. Our First Appointment Each Day

Robert gives an illustration of the Presidential Daily Briefing as the most important part of any given president's day. He then relates this to the importance of our meeting with the Lord each day.

APPLYING BALANCE: Although this pattern is called "maximize the morning", Rob notes that this daily devotional practice doesn't have to be in the morning (although this is tremendously helpful if it's possible, and you still shouldn't neglect his urge to begin the day in a spirit of prayer and praise). He says: "Your 'morning devotions' might happen during the lunch hour, at bedtime, or at some other regular spot on your daily agenda...The timing is flexible, but the habit isn't..."

EXPLORE: Read Proverb 8:34 and Matthew 6:6. How do these texts encourage you to pattern your daily schedule?

_____

_____

_____

_____

REFLECT: Do you have a daily time set aside for communion with God through prayer and Bible study, and is it consistent? Circle one:

YES / NO

APPLY: If your answer to the previous question was "yes", be sure it's part of your "Focus Block Chart" (from pattern two). If your answer was "no", spend some time with your "Focus Block Chart" from pattern two, incorporating this element into your schedule.

_____

_____

_____

_____

REFLECT: If you're currently having daily devotions, do you feel that they're helpful and consistent in their pattern? Are there areas where you struggle? Explain below:

_____

_____

_____

_____

APPLY: Pastor Morgan offers his own personal daily pattern for devotions. While yours can vary, I would make a personal note here to say—I have witnessed first-hand the consistent pattern of Rob's daily devotions, and the ways this habit transforms and empowers his days—carefully consider his method. If you're new to devotions, I'd recommend following his pattern exactly before you develop your own habits. If you're an old pro, compare notes and see how his habits can challenge or strengthen your own.

- Rob details how he identifies a *place* that's dedicated to his time with the Lord. He mentions ideas such as a secluded mountain vista, park bench, or walk along the beach. But he also mentions places as simple as a garage with faux walls making an area the size of a phone booth. The most important application is to *find a dedicated place for your time with the Lord.*

- He then details his pattern, which includes:

  - *Journaling*: Beginning with a short journal entry with a few notes about the previous or current day, and the passage he's studying.

  - *Prayer*: Rob utters a quick prayer asking the Lord to bless the rest of their time together.

  - *Bible Reading & Meditation*: He makes an important note here that he is "in no hurry to rush through a passage, so I may spend several days in the same paragraph. On other days I might read several chapters. My goal is finding some spiritual nourishment for the day…" He also mentions this time is often used for *Scripture memory*. This time typically takes him about ten to thirty minutes.

  - *Prayer*: This prayer is more extended than the previous "quick prayer" after journaling. As Robert says: "It helps to visualize the Lord Jesus close at hand and talk to Him as if He were really there—which, of course, He is." While not making this rote, Rob does use lists as a guide (but not a limitation) as to what to pray for and to recognize how the Lord has answered previous prayers.

  - *Singing a Hymn or Reading an Inspirational Book*: To close out his time in a spirit of prayer, Pastor Morgan will sing a hymn or gather some inspiration to take with him into his day.

  - One final item Rob addresses is an important component to weave together time with the Lord and managing your life— this final part of a daily devotional time is the subject of the entire next section.

APPLYING BALANCE: Although these devotional times are important and focused singularly on communion with God, Pastor Morgan makes a crucial note: "We mustn't segregate our sacred time from our secular lives. My point is, we're aided in our daily walk if we get it started on the right foot each morning."

APPLY: Rob ends this section with the appropriate challenge that I'd simply echo here, encouraging you to start tomorrow morning:

> *The Lord is more concerned about our walk with Him than our work for Him. Don't miss another day of fellowship with the Father...Plan ahead. Find a place...you have an appointment to keep. The God of the universe will be waiting on you, so don't be late.*

3. Before Leaving the Presence

In the previous section, we looked at Robert's daily devotional pattern, leaving off the final step, which is the focus of this section.

APPLY: As you finish up your quiet time, read these words from the book. Use the following paragraphs from the book as a guide to create your own four-by-six card or electronic document.

> *Here is the best system I've found for making sense of every day. Before I leave the conscious presence of God at the end of my morning quiet time, I take a few moments to look prayerfully at my lists of obligations and my calendar. On a little four-by-six card, I scratch out a plan. You can do this on an electronic device, of course. I use a card because I stick it in my pocket and carry it with me all day.*
>
> *After briefly considering my priorities and agenda, I got at the top of that card the one thing I most need to accomplish that day. Perhaps there are two or three things, but almost never more than three. I draw a box around them. In the space beneath I jot down anything else I need to remember about the day—perhaps a list of my appointments or other to-do items I should tackle if possible. On the back of the card, I usually write my current Bible memory verse.*
>
> *That becomes my plan for the day.*

REFLECT: The book gives several illustrations to highlight the importance of prioritizing our tasks. Why do you think prioritizing your day's agenda should be tacked on at the end of your time with the Lord?

_____

_____

_____

_____

APPLY: Take today's tasks and spend a brief time of prayer over them, re-prioritizing them with the wisdom God gives you.

_____

_____

_____

_____

APPLYING BALANCE: As we've noted several times, we can go too far with our task lists and priorities—becoming overly frustrated with delays or interruptions. Pastor Morgan offers this helpful comment:

> *Sometimes the interruptions represent the Father's business, as we learn by studying the life of Christ...sometimes the interruptions became His ministry...*

4. Try the Fifteen-Minute Plan

This section is only applicable if you don't currently have a consistent, daily devotional time with the Lord. If you've read this section, the challenge is quite simple.

APPLY: Set aside fifteen minutes per day as devotional time in the way Robert suggests:

1. Spend five minutes reading your Bible.

2. Spend five minutes in prayer.

3. Spend five minutes planning out your day.

**Another important note I would personally add to the book's 15 minute method has to do with meditation. Dr. Donald Whitney, a seminary professor of mine (and author of the excellent book "Spiritual Disciplines for the Christian Life"), argued that Christians most consistently neglect the practice of meditation on Scripture. When we don't meditate on Scriptures we've read, we often don't remember them or apply them throughout our day. I would personally take 1-2 minutes away from any section in the schedule offered above to meditate on what you've read after reading it.

Pattern Five:
PULL OFF AT REST STOPS

"...get some rest."
–Mark 6:31

"...take heed to yourselves..."
–Acts 20:28 (NKJV)

"The Lord has assigned to each his task"
–1 Corinthians 3:5

We've spent most of our time exploring the importance of accomplishing specific tasks according to God's purpose for our lives. It's important to note that God's divine purpose includes times of rest, relaxation, refueling, enjoyment, and other rejuvenating activities. However, it's easy for us neglect this practice, or at least to neglect understanding and applying the spiritual component of it. That's what we need to explore next.

Before moving on, read the fifth pattern from *Mastering Life Before It's Too Late.*

Robert breaks pattern five down into three main sections.

Let's look at each section:

1. Make Wise Withdrawals

EXPLORE: Read Mark 6:7–13 and verses 30–32. How does this story affect your approach to the work God has given you?

_____

_____

REFLECT: Pastor Morgan writes, "If we live in perpetual fatigue, it's time to bring a new rhythm into our hours, days, and weeks." I can personally recall many times over the past decade Rob has reminded me of this principle based on his perception of my mental or emotional state. How do you feel right now? Are you worn out, fatigued, exhausted? Describe your current state and how often you feel you could use scheduled times of rest:

_____

_____

_____

REFLECT: A good deal of this section cites Scriptures that show how frequently the Bible shows us Jesus' habit of "withdrawing" at key times. Does your life reflect this pattern? Why or why not? Explain your answer:

_____

_____

_____

_____

APPLY: This section sets us up for some key principles we'll discover in the next section to avoid burnout. Perhaps the most important takeaway in this section is that we grasp the importance of implementing a pattern of rest into our lives. Write a few specific ways you plan to incorporate this principle into your routine:

_____

_____

_____

_____

2. Take Heed to Yourself

EXPLORE: Read Acts 20:28. What's significant about the way this sentence is arranged? (*If you have trouble with the answer, Rob addresses this in the second paragraph of this section.*)

_____

_____

_____

_____

REFLECT: The book highlights several reasons fatigue is counterproductive. Circle the items you feel are true of you when you're tired:

  I'm less efficient

  My temper is shorter

  My schedule is more stress-filled

  My work feels heavier and less possible

  I feel unhealthy and, if sustained, I know this could shorten my life

EXPLORE: Notice the bullet points Robert gives with Scriptural references to the Lord's desire to give rest to His people. Why is this significant to you personally?

_____

_____

_____

_____

REFLECT: Pastor Morgan mentions that, for many of us, resting is an act of faith. It's always been this way. Rob cites Leviticus 16:29, speaking of the Sabbath, which says: "You must deny yourselves and not do any work". Is resting an activity of faith for you, in which you're purposely denying yourself the ability to "accomplish" something, and instead you focus on the provision and goodness of God? Explain your struggles and/or victories in this area:

_____

_____

_____

_____

EXPLORE: The book offers two important perspectives to avoid burnout. He tells us we need to rest our body (based on Mark 6:31). But he adds that we must rest our spirit as well. Read Matthew 11:28–29 and explain what resting in spirit means:

_____

_____

_____

_____

APPLY: After exploring these two perspectives to avoid burnout, Robert offers two practical ways his own life was changed. First, he made a list of corrective steps (i.e. taking a day off each week, not setting an alarm unless necessary, etc.). Secondly, Rob mentions that he implemented taking a Sabbath—a day off. He mentions that his Sabbath is on Saturday since Sunday, as a preacher, is a workday.

■ Make a list of your own "corrective" steps to get rid of overwork and implement rest:

_____

_____

_____

_____

■ What day of the week can you take a Sabbath? Write a plan or a prayer to purposely deny yourself work and to relax and trust the Lord on that day:

_____

_____

_____

_____

3. Do What Only You Can Do

In this section, the book emphasizes the importance of delegating tasks to others. How does this fit within the pattern of "pulling off at rest stops"? As we'll see from Biblical examples, when we delegate tasks we're not called to do, we greatly relieve our own burden.

EXPLORE: Read Exodus 18, then re-read verses 22 and 23. Why is this significant as you consider the work God has called you to?

_____

_____

_____

_____

EXPLORE: Read Acts 6:1–7 and answer the following questions:

■ What do verses 2 and 4 tell us about the apostles' motivation to delegate?

_____

_____

■ We often worry that delegating will offend others. How did the congregation react to this suggestion?

_____

_____

■ What was the result of delegating this work?

_____

_____

APPLY: Robert gives us two personal applications in this section.

■ First, we should ask ourselves this question: "What are the things that only I alone can do?" Rob gives several examples listed below. Add to this list things that only you can do:

  ○ Only you can be a husband or wife to your spouse.
  ○ Only you can be a parent to your children.
  ○ Only you can be a grandparent to those youngsters.
  ○ Only you can fill a unique role in the life of someone who is special to you.
  ○ Only you can nourish your soul and care for your body in a way that's pleasing to the Lord.
  ○ Only you can...

  ○ _____

  ○ _____

  ○ _____

  ○ _____

  ○ _____

- Second, we should ask the question Robert asks: "What am I currently doing that I can persuade, hire out, assign, delegate, or somehow shift to someone else—or release undone?" Make a list of those items below:

  ○ _____

  ○ _____

  ○ _____

  ○ _____

  ○ _____

  ○ _____

  ○ _____

  ○ _____

APPLY: Rob also encourages us to apply these principles to our family. If you're a parent, write out some ways below you can (or reflect on ways you already do) delegate tasks as chores.

_____

_____

_____

_____

_____

_____

_____

_____

The Sixth Pattern:
OPERATE ON YOURSELF

"Therefore we do not lose heart. Though outwardly we are wasting away, yet inwardly we are being renewed day by day."
–2 Corinthians 2:16

Before moving on, read the sixth pattern from *Mastering Life Before It's Too Late.*

This pattern includes one section entitled: *"The Art of Strengthening Yourself in the Lord."*

Let's look at this section:

To understand what Pastor Morgan means by *"Operate on Yourself: The Art of Strengthening Yourself in the Lord"*, let's look at how he describes it:

> *The art of strengthening oneself in the Lord is the greatest of all the spiritual disciplines. Sometimes, under the guidance of the Great Physician, we have to open ourselves up, take a look, improve ourselves, talk to ourselves, encourage ourselves, make our own changes, remove an infected attitude or an inflamed habit, and help ourselves become healthier.*

REFLECT: In Rob's description above and throughout the chapter, he gives several examples of being "infected" in need of self-surgery. Circle any of the items below that represent areas where you need surgery:

- Unhealthy attitudes

- Toxic habits

- Infectious sins

- Self-pity

- Embittering anger

- Despair

- Ingratitude

- Anxiety

EXPLORE: The book builds a biblical case for operating on ourselves / strengthening ourselves in the Lord. Look up and re-read the following passages in your Bible, or highlight and re-read them in this chapter of *Mastering Life*:

- 1 Samuel 30:6
- Psalm 62:5–6
- Psalm 103:1
- Lamentations 3:20–23

APPLY: Pastor Morgan describes this sort of self-surgery we see in Scripture as having three components: Reminding ourselves of God's promises, rekindling a sense of His presence, and preaching to ourselves His stalwart truths in troubled times. Following the example of the biblical writers, write a few lines to yourself that include these three components:

_____

_____

_____

_____

APPLY: Robert explains his own approach to self-surgery:

> *Whenever we're overwhelmed with something, either in our soul or our circumstances, we have to shut the door, open the Word, and search the Scriptures until we find a passage that helps us regain perspective.*

With this in mind, take the items you circled at the beginning of this section of the workbook that represent areas of surgery you need and re-write them below. Take some time to find and write memory verse(s) below the area you're battling. Keep in mind Rob's reminder that we should especially focus on the promises of God. For example:

- Toxic Habits – "Self Surgery" Verses

  - Galatians 5:16 – "So I say, walk by the Spirit, and you will not gratify the desires of the flesh."

  - 1 Corinthians 10:13 – "No temptation has overtaken you except what is common to mankind. And God is faithful; he will not let you be tempted beyond what you can bear. But when you are tempted, he will also provide a way out so that you can endure it."

_____

_____

_____

_____

_____

_____

_____

_____

APPLYING BALANCE: This section focuses on what the book calls "spiritual self-sufficiency". However, we're not created to live out our faith in isolation. It's an important biblical practice to learn the art of encouraging ourselves in the Lord, which is the focus of this chapter; but we shouldn't overlook the absolute necessity to live out our faith without other believers as an irreducible part of that equation. As Robert notes, 1 Samuel 23:16 tells us, *"Saul's son Jonathan went to David at Horesh and helped him find strength in God."* May we strive to build friendships like this, and to be friends like this!

The Seventh Pattern:
LIVE AS IF

"For as he thinks in his heart, so is he."
–Proverbs 23:7; NKJV

Before moving on, read the seventh pattern from *Mastering Life Before It's Too Late.*

This pattern includes one section entitled: *"Harness the Psychology of the Soul."*

Let's look at this section:

The "as if" principle is described as choosing our own attitude in any given set of circumstances. However, Rob adds: "Though the *as if* principle may be the basis for most of the self-improvement literature of the last century, to be truly effective, it needs a biblical anchor."

EXPLORE: Robert offers several Scriptures in this chapter to highlight what he calls the *as if* principle. Look up and re-read the following passages in your Bible, or highlight and re-read them in this chapter of your book and use the space below each to comment as to how this principle works itself out in the Bible:

■ Hebrews 11:27

_____

_____

■ Proverbs 23:7

_____

_____

■ 1 Corinthians 7:29–31

_____

_____

■ 1 Timothy 5:1

_____

_____

■ Hebrews 13:3

_____

_____

REFLECT: Pastor Morgan essentially says that everyone lives according to this principle, but there's a marked difference between believers and non-believers:

> _Too many people act **as if** there were no God, **as if** God didn't care about their lives or behavior, **as if** God's promises weren't true. But Christians have the unspeakable joy of dealing with **as ifs** that are realities...We persevere **as if** seeing Him who is invisible._

Which set of _as if_ statements above caricaturize your behavior in the past week? How can applying the Scriptures in the above "**EXPLORE**" section modify your attitudes and behaviors?

_____

_____

_____

_____

APPLY: Robert makes several suggestions towards the end of this chapter. Choose and highlight an _as if_ statement below and make a commitment to apply it today:

- We claim the promises of God _as if_ they were real—which they are

- We obey the commands of God _as if_ they were urgent—which they are

- We view circumstances _as if_ God were on His throne—which He is

- We determine to adopt biblical attitudes like love, joy, peace, patience, kindness, and peace, even when we don't feel like it.

APPLYING BALANCE: This pattern can be taken too far, to a level of exhaustion. While we've looked primarily at _as if_ Scriptures, there are also many Scriptures that encourage us to embrace, experience, and work through our emotions. This principle can, as Rob says, "at worst [result in] too-eager salesmen and health-and-wealth preachers...it can also spawn artificiality and hypocrisy." Rob also includes a story about his wife, Katrina, who became exhausted trying to over-apply this principle. Be sure to apply this principle as it's laid out in Scripture, balanced with authenticity.

The Eighth Pattern:
BATHE IN THE DEAD SEA

"...I will rejoice in the Lord, I will be joyful in God my Savior."
–Habakkuk 3:18

Before moving on, read the eighth pattern (all three sections) from Mastering Life Before It's Too Late.

Robert breaks pattern eight down into three main sections, all centered around cultivating joy in our lives.

Let's look at each section:

1. The Singular Secret of Unsinkable Saints

REFLECT: Pastor Morgan explains that, like floating in the Dead Sea, true joy gives us buoyancy. However, we often face overwhelming circumstances like Jeremiah who said, "The waters closed over my head, and I thought I was about to perish" (Lamentations 3:54). Do you feel this way now? If so, describe your situation and how you feel in the midst of it:

_____

_____

_____

_____

EXPLORE: The same Jeremiah who wrote the words in Lamentations also wrote: *"Your words were found, and I ate them, and Your word was to me the joy and rejoicing of my heart"* (Jeremiah 15:16). Why was it possible for the same man to write both Scriptures?

_____

_____

_____

_____

REFLECT: The book offers five principles and corresponding Scriptures to build a biblical view of joy. Write your personal response to each below. For example: "God's home is a joyful place, so despite my difficult family situation I can be thankful that the world isn't my home."

- God's very personality is full of joy.

_____

_____

- God's home is a joyful place.

_____

_____

- We should pay attention to the joy God has woven into all His creation.

_____

_____

- Jesus came to reinstate joy to His creation.

_____

_____

- Christians have a sacred obligation to live joyfully.

_____

_____

APPLYING BALANCE: Robert warns us not to take this idea further than we should:

> *This doesn't mean we are always ecstatic and gleeful. The heroes of the Bible displayed a full range of emotions, and Jesus wept by the tomb of His friend Lazarus. None of us knows what may befall us day by day, and the joy of the Lord doesn't rescind all heartache.*

APPLY: Rob argues that joy "doesn't cancel the difficult moments of life, but it does transcend life's circumstances." Below, write the biggest difficulty you face. Then, below it, write the words: "Sorrowful, yet always rejoicing...In all our troubles my joy knows no bounds" (2 Corinthians 6:10, 7:4).

_____

_____

_____

_____

EXPLORE: Read Habakkuk 3:17–19. Notice the honest expression of difficulty in this passage, but not without a statement of trust in the Lord at the end. Why is this significant?

_____

_____

_____

_____

APPLY: Many Psalms we call "Lament Psalms" follow this pattern (Read Psalm 4 for an example.). Take a moment to write out your own personal "lament psalm", but below it write a statement of trust in the Lord despite your troubles:

_____

_____

_____

_____

_____

_____

_____

_____

2. The Executive Joy of Pleasantly Productive Leadership

EXPLORE: Pastor Morgan recounts the story of David in 2 Samuel 18 and 19. Read these chapters and note 19:5–7. What does this teach us about leadership?

_____

_____

_____

_____

APPLYING BALANCE: Robert notes (about the passage above):

> *This is the Spirit-disciplined attitude. It's not just a matter of stoicism or fatalism; nor does it involve being bubbly and fizzy…having an effervescent personality…It's the reflection of a stewarded sense of thankful joy that runs deeply and quietly through the hearts of God's best leaders…It can't be faked, but it can be cultivated.*

REFLECT: Rob reminds us, "joy and gloom are both contagious". In what situations are you currently spreading a bad attitude? In what situations are you spreading positivity? Explain below:

_____

_____

_____

_____

_____

_____

_____

APPLY: Pastor Morgan argues, "Pleasantly productive leaders harness the power of biblical joy…To be joyfully thankful is the foundation of influence…That's executive joy, and that creates the environment for effective leadership." To help us cultivate joy, Pastor Morgan explains that biblical leadership follows a three-part biblical pattern as it pertains to joy.

Below each of these three principles, re-word each verse in personal action language. For example, under Proverbs 15:13 you might write: *"It's important that I cultivate joy not only for myself, but so others will see and be affected by my disposition."*

1. Transforming Joy:

Proverbs 15:13 — *"A happy heart makes a cheerful face"*

_____

_____

_____

_____

2. Transcendent Joy:

Proverbs 15:15 — "A cheerful heart has a continual feast"

_____

_____

_____

_____

3. Transferrable Joy:

Proverbs 15:30 — "A cheerful look brings joy to the heart of others"

_____

_____

_____

_____

3. Well Versed in Happiness:

In this section, Robert writes:

> *The thing that makes some people happier is that they have found something to be substantially happy about, and they have learned to cultivate that attitude like a farmer tending prize-winning crops.*

He then argues that Scripture memory and meditation are key in cultivating happiness, citing Psalm 19:8: *"The precepts of the Lord are right, giving joy to the heart".*

APPLY: The majority of this section of the book is Scripture verses and notes. Rob himself challenges us to apply these Scriptures:

> *Here, then, are some verses to chew on, which I'm listing and quoting below with a few observations about each. Select some of these and commit them to memory. Find one to quote aloud every morning and evening for the next month. Post it on your dashboard or desk.*

Use your book to find & select verses.

The Ninth Pattern:
PRACTICE THE POWER OF PLODDING

"'Not by might nor by power, but by My Spirit,' says the Lord almighty...
Who dares despise the day of small things?"
–Zechariah 4:6, 10

Before moving on, read the ninth pattern from Mastering Life Before It's Too Late.

This pattern includes one section entitled: "Don't Despise the Day of Small Things."

Let's look at this section:

REFLECT: I've personally witnessed believers approaching Rob, discouraged that they've not accomplished something world changing. His response to them is the same he writes here:

> *I'm convinced we're too enamored of the dramatically big when most of life is blessedly small. Sometimes we mistakenly equate smallness with insignificance, but that's an indictment against God's wisdom in planning our ways.*

What "big things" in life are you discouraged about not being fulfilled? In what ways do your efforts feel insignificant? Do you think God has the same perspective? Explain below:

_____

_____

_____

_____

EXPLORE: Read Haggai 2:1–9. Summarize God's perspective on rebuilding the temple in a couple of sentences below:

_____

_____

_____

REFLECT: Pastor Morgan points out that it's easier to plot than to plod, but both are necessary. Do you see yourself as more of a plotter or a plodder? Should you give more attention to either area? Explain below:

_____

_____

_____

_____

APPLY: Think of a big endeavor, even a life-long goal, you're working in small steps to accomplish. Are you realizing it's not worth the effort and need to abandon it? If so, write your reasoning below and a brief prayer, relinquishing it into God's hands:

_____

_____

_____

_____

APPLY: On the other hand, have you decided to push forward in this endeavor despite difficulty or discouragement? If so, choose one of the two following Bible verses to memorize as a sort of banner to hang over your endeavor:

> *I will give you every place where you set your foot…Do not be discouraged, for the Lord your God will be with you wherever you go. (Joshua 1:3, 9)*

> *Be strong and courageous, and do the work. Do not be afraid or discouraged, for the Lord God, my God, is with you. He will not fail you or forsake you until all the work for the service of the temple of the Lord is finished. (1 Chronicles 28:20)*

EXPLORE: As you "plod" through the small tasks that represent major pursuits, Robert argues that the biblical quality of perseverance is vital. Look up and read the following verses or find them in this chapter of the book and highlight them. Make notes below each as to how they apply in your situation:

■ *1 Corinthians 13:7*

_____

_____

■ *1 Timothy 4:16*

_____

_____

■ *Hebrews 10:36, 12:11*

_____

_____

■ *James 1:12, 5:11*

_____

_____

Pattern Ten:
REMEMBER THERE ARE TWO OF YOU

"I have been crucified with Christ and I no longer live, but Christ lives in me. The life I now live in the body, I live by faith in the Son of God, who loved me and gave himself for me."
–Galatians 2:20

Before moving on, read the tenth pattern from Mastering Life Before It's Too Late.

Robert breaks pattern ten down into three main sections.

Let's look at each section:

1. Double Vision

EXPLORE: Read Galatians 2:20. How should this impact your approach to the work God has given you to accomplish?

_____

_____

_____

_____

EXPLORE: Read John 15 and Galatians 5:22–23. Write a few sentences summarizing the analogy Jesus gives of Himself as the vine and us as branches. Explain, based on Galatians 5, the resulting fruit:

_____

_____

_____

_____

REFLECT: Would you confidently say you produce the kind of fruit listed in Galatians 5:22–23? If not, explain how that may relate to your being reliant on Christ as the Vine:

_____

_____

_____

_____

EXPLORE: Pastor Morgan lists nine passages in bullet points to discuss the significance of the word _through_ in Scripture. Summarize the significance of this word below:

_____

_____

_____

_____

APPLY: Rob asks the question, "In practical terms, how does this work? Well, in a sense, that's the scope of this entire book with all ten of its core principles…" He summarizes the action steps needed to live a Christ-indwelled and Spirit-empowered life. Review them here and in the book for a fuller description, writing notes below each as to how you have or plan to implement them:

- First, we must freely acknowledge the lordship of Christ over every area of life. We must surrender to Him every corner, crevice, and closet.

  _____

  _____

- Second…we should meet the Lord each morning [or each day] and as we do so we can ask Him to fill us afresh with His Holy Spirit.

  _____

  _____

- Third, we must envision this process in the most realistic terms possible and claim the experience by faith.

_____

_____

APPLY: The book offers some very practical ways we can apply the principle of Christ's indwelling presence and power. Highlight the ones that apply to you specifically and add more below, committing each item to Christ in faith that His indwelling will enable you:

- I'm not trying to sign up this new client; Jesus is doing that.
- I'm not raising my child; Jesus is doing it through me.
- I can't solve this problem; Jesus will give wisdom…
- I'm not trying to control my temper, I'm saying, "Lord, Your patience, please."
- I'm not trying to bear this burden, I can cast it in the Lord's hands and claim His peace.
- I'm not the one who will save this soul. That's the Lord's part of the work.
- I don't have the strength to clean this house, transport this van of kids, prepare this meal, or coach this soccer team. But if this is what the Lord wants me to do today, strength will rise as I wait upon Him.
- I'm not trying to launch this business. I'm saying, "Lord as I seek to build my business, I ask Your will to be done with it, here on earth, just as Your will is done in heaven."

- _____
  _____

- _____
  _____

- _____
  _____

- _____
  _____

- _____
  _____

2. God's Arithmetic

REFLECT: The primary point of this section, Rob summarizes this way:

> *When He works through us by His Spirit, He takes our words and works, folds them over, and blesses them...their impact is like the ripple of a pond that expands through time in increasingly wide circles until it reaches the shores of eternity.*

He then lists several tasks we often overlook, assuming to be insignificant, yet often begin (sometimes unknown to us) a chain reaction for God's glory. The tasks Rob mentions are below—circle each one you've accomplished in your life:

- Perform a good deed

- Speak a meaningful word

- Pray for a friend

- Train up a child

- Tutor a youngster

- Distribute a Bible

- Share a testimony

- Teach a lesson

- Support a ministry

Take a moment to ponder how God may very well have multiplied your efforts.

REFLECT: Galatians 6:9 tells us, "Let us not become weary in doing good, for at the proper time we will reap a harvest if we do not give up." Are you weary or exhausted from the work God has assigned you? If so, how does this verse encourage you or affect you?

_____

_____

_____

_____

EXPLORE: Robert points out the shift of the mathematical term from addition to multiplication in the book of Acts. Why is this significant? What evidence is there that this principle has remained true throughout church history? Explain below:

_____

_____

_____

_____

_____

APPLY: Write a prayer below, committing particular "small things" to the Lord, dedicating yourself to accomplishing small tasks and trusting God to multiply your work.

_____

_____

_____

_____

3. Pipelines of Grace

If you've made it this far in the book, and in the workbook, you might still somehow feel discouraged. That's why Pastor Morgan ends the book with this section, saying: "Perhaps you've tried and failed too many times. Maybe you've stumbled, fallen, and, in discouragement, decided to lie in the leaves rather than rediscover the path."

EXPLORE: Read Proverbs 24:16. How does this speak to your feelings of discouragement?

_____

_____

_____

_____

REFLECT: After reading Robert's story in this section, do you resonate with any of these statements he makes? If so, highlight them below:

- Maybe you've had a terrible fall

- Perhaps you've made a mistake

- Maybe you've fallen into sin

- Maybe your plans have fallen apart like a cheap contraption

- Perhaps a sense of frustration or failure haunts you, even a sense of futility

APPLY: The final challenge Rob gives is to anyone who's experiencing this kind of discouragement:

> *But the Lord Jesus Christ was lifted up and crucified to provide all the forgiveness you need. If you'll pick yourself up right now and determine to make the best use of the path ahead, you'll find that the heavenly Father has a pipeline of grace running right by your footsteps.... If you'll give everything to Him, He will lead you to the reservoirs of His strength. If you follow the pipelines of His grace, they will lead you home.*

FINAL NOTES

I pray this workbook has been helpful in guiding you to dig deeper into Scripture, to reflect and ponder your own life authentically, and especially to make lasting and meaningful commitments.

If you've found Robert's writing helpful, and have enjoyed individual or group study, you might consider other group study resources available at ***robertjmorgan.com***

- The Red Sea Rules takes readers on a journey from panic to praise through applying principles from Exodus 14 and 15 as God led the Israelites through the Red Sea. A printed 10-week study guide is available, as well as a free downloadable facilitator's guide.

- The Lord is My Shepherd walks readers through Psalm 23 verse by verse. As you travel through green pastures and still waters, as you encounter the valley of the shadow of death—through all the twists and turns of life you'll learn what it means to truly follow the Good Shepherd. A printed 10-week study guide is available, as well as a free downloadable facilitator's guide.

- 100 Bible Verses Everyone Should Know is a collection of the verses Robert J. Morgan has compiled to challenge his church, his children and grandchildren, and you. Grouped into similar themes with exposition and teaching, Robert walks through these life-altering verses and offers helpful memory techniques along the way. A facilitator's guide is available, as well as additional free downloads.

MASTERING

LIFE

STUDY GUIDE

Robert J. Morgan Books
615-846-6222
RobertJMorgan.com

CPSIA information can be obtained
at www.ICGtesting.com
Printed in the USA
LVHW050749170519
618152LV00003B/3/P